Also by Ronald Hirsch

The Self in No Self: Buddhist Heresies and Other Lessons of a Buddhist Life

Making Your Way in Life as a Buddhist: A Practical Guide

Scratching the Itch: Getting to the Root of Our Suffering

We STILL Hold These Truths: Preserving the Heart of American Democracy for the 21st Century

Raising a Happy Child

A Practical Guide

Ronald Hirsch

ThePracticalBuddhist.com Publishing

Published 2013 by ThePracticalBuddhist.com Publishing, Stuyvesant, NY 12173. U.S. © 2012 Ronald L. Hirsch. All rights reserved.

ISBN 978-0-9883290-6-5 (softcover), 978-0-9883290-7-2 (eBook)

To all the children in the world, whether rich or poor,
who suffer from feelings of insecurity and unhappiness
and to the unhappy, insecure adults that they become.
May they grow up instead happy and secure.

TABLE OF CONTENTS

Preface

The myth of childhood is that it is a happy, carefree time. While it may be true that most children are free of the burdens of the adult world that is not to say that their lives are either carefree or happy.

Even before the contemporary madness that places huge stress on the children of upper-middle and upper income parents to succeed and the well-publicized phenomenon of "mean girls" and school bullies, children were subjected to an abundance of stresses. These stresses derived partly from their interaction with family and partly from the culture of children, which not surprisingly mimics the culture of adults and can be very cruel.

Children ask the same questions of themselves as do adults … who am I, am I loved, am I desired, am I attractive, am I smart, etc. … perhaps with even greater urgency because their egos, their sense of self, is less formed. And as in the case of adults, children seek these answers from their family, their peers, and the culture around them. For many if not most, the answers they get back are negative or at best equivocal.

A *New Yorker* cartoon reflects this unfortunate reality. It shows a mother sitting on her young son's bed with her arm around him saying, "Heavens no, sweetie – my love for you has tons of conditions."[1] Obviously this is usually not stated so bluntly, but it is nevertheless clearly communicated through a parent's actions and words and definitely felt by the child. Unconditional love and compassion is unfortunately rarely present in the relationship between parent and child.

---

[1] E. F. Lake, *The New Yorker*, June 6, 2011, p.55

Even if the answers they get back are positive ... that they are attractive or smart, for example ... children fear that they will loose that quality in the future or that someone may outdo them resulting in their losing their position in their immediate society's pecking order. The consequence is a world full of insecure, unhappy children who become insecure, unhappy adults.

Children and adults may learn to mask their insecurity with humor, bluster or bravado, but they are nevertheless deeply insecure because they have no knowledge of themselves beyond what others think of them. Even, or perhaps especially, those most successful in our society ... celebrities, corporate titans, financial wizards, real estate moguls ... are victims of this cultural phenomenon because they have so much to lose, which is why they are so often notoriously imperious and difficult. Or why even celebrated actors and performers get butterflies in their stomach before going onstage; it represents a fear that most people never completely lose.

This is not to say that children and adults do not experience moments of happiness or are not able to laugh or be light-spirited. The point is that the underlying emotions that are in our guts are typically insecurity and unhappiness.

How did we come to this point? How with all the progress we have made in so many areas of life do we produce generation after generation of insecure, unhappy children and adults?

The answer in one sense is very straightforward. It's a function both of our culture ... what it values and the way we treat each other ... and the fact that insecure adults will in almost all likelihood raise insecure children.

There is little one can do about the culture that surrounds us. It is what it is, although being aware of its impact on us provides an opening to free ourselves of that impact. But one can, I believe, change the cycle of insecure parents raising insecure children. And that is the goal of this book.

To those of you who will respond, "I'm not insecure and unhappy," I say look deeply inside yourself ... if you can ... and unless you are the rare exception you will see someone who is, regarding some important aspects of your being, insecure and unhappy. It is this insecurity and unhappiness/frustration that drives you to do much of what you do, both in the work environment and elsewhere. But in our culture, it is not a desirable trait to be insecure or unhappy. One certainly doesn't talk about it. And so most of us learn early on to put on a façade of being happy and secure, regardless how we are feeling inside. In time we not only take refuge in that façade but we come to believe in it as reflective of who we are.

Some of you may say, "This is a bunch of rubbish. These problems are not caused by our culture or by parents, this is just the human condition." I would say in response that while it is certainly true that emotions such as fear, panic, and aggression are inherent in humans and part of our evolutionary biological heritage, those basic emotions have morphed and expanded exponentially as human culture has become increasingly urbanized and less communal.

In the post-industrial revolution era, as we have become part of an increasingly rootless, mobile society and culture based largely on the promotion of consumerism and competition, these emotions have become a major part of how we function on a daily basis ... to the point that they define us. Throughout our life cycle we are bombarded with images of what traits are desirable and which aren't, of what we need to have to maintain a certain image. To answer the question, "Who am I?" is to look into a kaleidoscopic mirror that reflects our culture's values. The result is insecurity and frustration ... an obsession with what we don't have and with the future. This is *not* the human condition.

This book, however, does not advocate withdrawing from our culture. This is our country; this is, for better or worse, the culture we live in. The goal is to find a way to interact with and be a part of the larger culture while retaining a perspective that is independent of it and our learned experience, allowing us to experience happiness, peace, and contentment.

This book posits that while we are born with an innate temperament that remains part of us till we die and a multitude of genetic predispositions, what becomes of our lives is overwhelmingly a function of learned experience ... what we learn/observe from our family, our peers, and the larger culture. What is commonly called the "nurture factor." Whether we become famous or a dropout, a doctor or a maintenance man, an addict or sober, a depressed person or a happy one ... all of this depends mostly on our life-experiences.

This certainly is true of our emotional state. And even in those areas where we have talent that is to some extent genetically based ... whether it's musical, mathematics, or artistic talent, or a high IQ ... what happens with that innate talent is totally a function of whether and how those seeds are nurtured.

A child is a fragile, vulnerable person. From the moment the child leaves the womb, and even before, a child is deeply and permanently impacted by his parents' changing moods as the child is totally dependent on those around him for sustenance and nurturing.

Every child has the potential to live a happy, wholesome, constructive, and fulfilling life.[2] Every child deserves a happy life. If a child does not experience that, it is mostly a function of its environment. Whether a result of

---

[2] We know today that even children born with a variety of birth/genetic defects can live happy, fulfilling lives.

some neglect, some lack of love, occasional physical or verbal abuse, or the negative impact of peers and the surrounding culture, such experiences have a definite impact on a child's psychological development.

The vast majority of parents are good people and want only the best for their child. They do not do anything intentionally to harm their child or decrease his or her potential.

But parents are people who are a function of their own upbringing and learned experience. They have their own fears, frustrations, angers, and desires. They see things through the lens of that experience and those emotions, which filters and often distorts reality which in turn has a negative impact on their interaction with their children, as well as others.

It is the goal of this book to provide parents with the means to step outside themselves, to be able to experience their child, themselves, and the culture around them mostly free of these emotions. Then parents will be able to provide their child with the love, nurturing, and direction it needs to be a happy child ... and at the same time help themselves find more peace and happiness.

Regardless at which stage of the process you are ... thinking about having a baby, pregnant, or already have a young or older child or even an adult child ... the suggestions contained in this book are relevant to your child's happiness and emotional security.

Chapter 1
To Have a Child or Not

In discussing how to raise a happy child, I am begging an important question ... which is, whether or not to have a child. That decision is one of the most impactful decisions that a man and woman will make in their lives, both on their lives and of course on the child who will be born. Yet all too often this decision is made for the wrong reasons, even if there is a frank reasoned discussion about it.

If you want to raise a happy, emotionally secure child, there are three questions that should be answered positively by prospective parents before trying to become pregnant and have a child. The first is, do both of you truly want to have a child? Several caveats are necessary.

Note that I said "both of you." Parenting is a joint responsibility and it brings with it plenty of stresses on the marital relationship. If the woman really wants to have a baby and the man feels ambivalent but is willing to go along to please her, that's not good enough. For the sake of your future child's and your happiness, both of you must be equally committed to having a child.

Couples are often under a lot of peer or family pressure to have a child. All their friends are having children. Both mothers of the couple keep asking when they're going to have a grandchild. As relentless as this pressure may be, pleasing others or being part of your group is not a good enough reason for having a child.

If you both truly want a child, the second question is ... are both of you ready to make the commitment necessary to give your child the attention and nurturing it will need in order to grow up happy and emotionally secure?

While many couples would likely answer this question with an easy, "yes," this is not a "duh" question.

The problem is that since such childrearing is not the norm, most couples have not experienced what it entails or feels like. Some couples react to this by saying, "What was good enough for me is good enough for my child." To the extent that they are aware of ways in which their upbringing was lacking, other couples answer this question by saying that they are committed to giving their child what they did not get as a child ... whether it's various resources, love and affection, attention, etc. With regards to their child's emotional needs, however, as heartfelt as that commitment may be, it is wanting because the couple typically doesn't really understand what the commitment entails ... it is not a knowing commitment.

After reading this book, however, both prospective parents will have an understanding of what will be required. Then you will be able to answer this question in a meaningful way.

The third question, while strictly speaking not relevant to whether your child grows up happy, is relevant to the happiness and fate of the human race and thus also of your child ... it is a question of social responsibility. We live in a world with an ever-expanding population (with the exception of a few western European countries) that is taking an ever-greater toll on the earth's environment. And even with technological advances, it is reaching or is already beyond the point where the earth's resources are not sufficient to sustain the population.

This question is especially relevant if you already have two children, which is roughly the average number of childbirths per couple necessary to maintain a population. In this case, even assuming that you both truly want a child and after reading this book feel you can make the commitment necessary to raise a healthy and emotionally secure child, you should seriously consider not having another child.

I would suggest that even if a couple is in a financial position to assure that their child would want for nothing, as a member of the broader society and a resident of this Earth, the socially responsible decision would be to not have another child. Population growth has to stop someplace, and that place is family planning decisions.

I understand that what I am suggesting is not part of the American discussion regarding family planning, but it needs to be. Regardless which issue of advancing shortage one looks at ... but especially water, energy, and food ... conservation is not enough, even if undertaken seriously, to solve the problem. What is needed in addition is a halt to population growth, as well as other things that are beyond the framework of this book.

But I digress. Raising a child can be a wondrous, rewarding experience or it can be hell or anywhere in between. Many parents would say that the difference is the result of the nature of the child. I obviously would argue that the difference lies mostly in the atmosphere in which the child was raised, starting from its time in the womb.

Chapter 2
Preparing for Parenthood

Go to any bookstore, and you will find a multitude of books about childrearing. And there are many parents who are conscientious about reading such books and applying the principles they contain. But these books are about the technique of raising a child … everything from the use of pacifiers to toilet training to stimulating the mind to applying praise and discipline to not overindulging to not micromanaging and to achieving success.

The problem with these books is typically threefold. First, they deal largely with outcomes, some important some on the periphery of life. While these factors do have an impact on your child's development, they do not deal directly with the health of your child's mind and soul...what a child regardless of its stage of development needs from a parent to grow up happy and secure...without which a healthy outcome, as opposed to a culturally approved outcome, is less likely to flow. Second, they generally do not question the prevailing culture, except as it pertains to child rearing. And that, as the preface indicates, is a major problem in raising a happy child. Third, they assume that parents can apply these principles with robot-like perfection. But parents are far from unemotional robots. You have your own mood swings, insecurities, and learned experience that impact both how your child is observed and interpreted and your reaction.

Everyone has experienced the fact that a father's and mother's attitude towards a child will often differ. The common explanation for this difference in approach is the difference between male and female psychologies. While that is undoubtedly to some extent true, the impact of their learned experience is far more important. Indeed, even the male/female difference is to a large extent a function of learned experience and culture, rather than biological.

To prepare you for parenthood, this book will proceed in a different manner. First it will ask the question, "What does it mean for a child or an adult to be happy, and how does our culture impact their ability to be happy." Second, it will ask the question, "How can you, the parent, step outside your experience and find your own peace and happiness so that you can see the unfiltered reality of your child at all times and enabling you to provide it with the nurturing it needs, apply your chosen child-raising techniques accurately and consistently, and pass your peace and happiness on to your child?" Third, the book will provide suggestions of how to address critical issues at various stages of your child's development, all founded on the answers to these questions.

WHAT DOES IT MEAN TO BE HAPPY?

Right from the start, this question exposes the rift between our culture and ones happiness.[3] For most people, what it means to be happy is defined by ones culture and learned experience, which although totally understandable is not a good thing if it does not in fact produce happiness.

In our culture, happiness is primarily defined by advertising and media images as having the financial ability to acquire the things that make for the "good" life. The more money one has and therefore the greater ability to acquire things, the happier one will be. Likewise, to be poor, to not have the ability to acquire the accoutrements of the good life, is to be unhappy.

This partly explains the fascination of so many people with the lives of the rich and famous. They live vicariously through the exalted state of these people. It also explains why even some poor people buy iconic (and expensive) brand-name consumer goods that provide them with some status.

Yet as any psychologist can attest, happiness does not derive from the accumulation of material things. It certainly results in a level of material comfort, but that does not equate with happiness. Furthermore, our cultural obsession or addiction with acquiring things, consuming, leads to high levels of dissatisfaction, frustration, and depression. When someone always wants what one doesn't have, or more of what one does have, there may be momentary periods where acquiring something or reaching a certain status brings a sense of satisfaction, but that passes rather quickly

---

[3] I should note at the outset that I am approaching this question, and indeed the entire book, from the perspective of a Buddhist. But regardless whether you are a Christian, Jew, or Muslim, or practice another religion, the message of this book is supported by the underlying values of your religion. It's our culture that is in conflict with the values of our religions.

as the ego-mind focuses on the next thing one needs to acquire to fulfill its craving and thus comes the inevitable frustration.

Related to the myth that having many things brings happiness, is the obsession among many people with higher education of achieving not just wealth, but the status and power that comes with wealth. Being looked up to by others, being envied, and having power over others is supposed to bring increased happiness. But we know that that is also a myth.

In former decades, the other cultural myth of achieving happiness was being a husband or wife in a family with children, the number of children changing as the decades passed. But we know that while in former decades the stability of marriage did bring with it security, especially financial, for women, the institution of marriage frequently did not equate with much happiness for either husband or wife. People made the best of things, but that is hardly happiness. Life was not like the iconic 1950s family sit-coms.

Today, with a divorce rate hovering around 50%, marriage often provides neither security nor happiness and increasing numbers of women are choosing to not get married and even have their children out of wedlock. This does not mean that these women have now found happiness, just that they don't have to deal with the particular problems of sharing their lives with men, whether they love them or not.

So if the two shibboleths of happiness in our culture … success/wealth and marriage … are in fact not good predictors of happiness, then what is happiness? There is a Buddhist saying that, "Happiness comes from within." That means that it does not spring from nor is dependent on anything external to oneself. On the contrary, such dependence only causes frustration and unhappiness.

Indeed, happiness can be said to be the lack of frustration that results from a sense of peace and contentment with the way things are right now at this moment. We arrive at that state of happiness by accepting our lives and ourselves as we are at this moment and having unconditional love and compassion for ourselves and others.

This does not mean that one is a slug, that one just vegetates, that one has no desires or ambitions. What it does mean is that one does not obsess about these things. One goes about ones days doing the best one can to achieve ones goals. If things go well, great. If things do not go well, it's not the end of the world. It means dwelling in a state of equanimity.

All of this runs counter to all the messages we receive from our culture and our learned experience. This is not what our ego tells us.

Indeed, for many people, the whole idea of acceptance and many of the other concepts I have discussed is downright scary. It's beyond our experience and so the fear of the unknown takes hold of us. But although our culture doesn't promote this way of thinking, these ideas go back thousands of years and can be found in almost every major religion and spiritual tradition. This is not new age strangeness; it is based on simple common sense.

If what I've said makes sense to you and you can see yourself and others in what I've said, then the question is, how does your child achieve this kind of happiness.

But before you as a parent can foster this type of happiness in your children, you must find it for yourself; otherwise your insecurities and frustrations and culture-laden view of the world will be passed on to your children. As stated earlier, the answer I'm suggesting is not to withdraw from our culture, but rather to find a way to have a perspective of yourself and the world around you that is independent of that culture and your learned experience, thus allowing you and your child to experience peace, contentment, and happiness.

FINDING HAPPINESS IN YOURSELF

Most of us go through our days ... each and every one ... focused on if not consumed by our worries, concerns, fears, anger, frustration, and desires ... consumed by our ego. And these emotional states color our reaction not just to everything that happens around us, but to ourselves. Think of the interactions you've had today with yourself and the world around you, be it your family, colleagues, strangers, or the broader world. Would you say your reactions have come from a place of peace and contentment, or have they come from one of the above—mentioned emotions?

If you want to exercise your best judgment in your interactions, you should not allow your judgment to be influenced by these emotions because they keep you from seeing things as they are and from acting in a manner which best furthers your interests ... both regarding yourself and those you are interacting with. So while finding peace, contentment, and happiness certainly has great spiritual value, it has immense practical value as well.

But how do we change this ingrained habit-energy of ours? Many years ago my life was consumed by these same distorting emotions. My life may have looked very successful both professionally and personally, but I was a very unhappy person under the façade I had created. And the teaching I was getting at temple really wasn't helping much.

So I slowly started building my own platform of peace and happiness based on the steps outlined in the following pages. It is a practical, realizable approach. It speaks to the goal of enabling one to begin experiencing peace, happiness, and hope in the present and from that contented space being able to exercise your judgment in all areas of your life with greater clarity and benefit ... especially in relationship to your child.

Mind you, since we are talking about changing habit-energies that have developed in you over several decades, the change will not occur overnight. It will require commitment, patience, and discipline. But the life-changing benefit to your child and to yourself cannot be overstated.

The Power of Smiling Mindfully

Most of us are frustrated or at least concerned about many aspects of our lives, both large and small. I did not *want* to accept things as being the way they are ... even for a moment. Yet I knew I had to take some steps to begin to bring some lightness into my life. The first step towards lessening the frustration we feel is to smile mindfully.[4]

As you go through the day, try to be aware of your facial expression. If you're like me, you'll find that in general your facial muscles are either frowning or in a serious repose. This is our usual state when we're alone with our thoughts as opposed to being engaged in conversation with others or being entertained.

Generally we frown for various reasons ... our culture is so focused on wanting what we don't have (not necessarily something material) and on proving ourselves through competition, we are so attached to the past and obsessed with the future, and the problems of the world around us are so vexing that most of us are in an almost constant state of some degree of frustration or concern, whether consciously or not. If we are frustrated, we are not happy, and that agitation shows in our facial expression.

Even when we get our lives more together and find some peace and happiness, we still frown because it is a default position that's a product of decades of negative muscle training brought about by a stressful life. I know

---

[4] The word "mindful" is used here as in its Buddhist context. It means to be aware, rather than experiencing and reacting to things automatically.

17

from my baby photos and family anecdotes that before I was burdened by my ego and learned experience I always had a smile on my face. My father called me his "sunshine."

I regret that it was only after years of Buddhist practice that I became aware one day that most of the time my facial muscles were tense. And as I observed my tense facial muscles, I became aware that this tenseness created a state of non-joy that overrode any sense of peace and contentment that I may have otherwise been feeling.

Purposefully, I brought a smile to my face and found much to my surprise that this in turn brought an immediate uplift to my spirits. Just releasing the facial tension made me feel lighter and filled with happiness. This is what Thich Nhat Hanh[5] calls "mouth yoga." But I found that the smile and its impact were fleeting because it was mechanical and I was quickly distracted.

Then one day while meditating,[6] I realized that if I were able to be aware every moment of the wonderful things in my life right then at each moment, I would smile mindfully and naturally every moment. Even if I was focused on some concern of mine, I would at the same time be mindful of the things that brought joy to my life.

Well, every moment was perhaps too much to expect at the start. But whenever during the course of the day I stopped for a moment's reflection (something one should do as often as possible), I would say to myself, "I am grateful for all the wonderful things in my life right now at this moment," and as those things came to mind I could feel myself smiling. As time passed, I observed that my awareness of the good things in my life began to permeate

---

[5] Thich Nhat Hanh is a well-respected Vietnamese Buddhist monk with a word-wide following.

[6] Yes, as a Buddhist I meditate every day. And I highly recommend the practice regardless of your religion. It is of great benefit. But that's the subject of other books, not this one.

my day and I smiled more, not just when I was in a reflective pause.

Of course this practice of smiling mindfully did not change my underlying condition or the reality of the world with its problems. But it did provide me with a renewed focus on the positive in my life and increased my experience of joy and happiness.

Taking Joy In Each Moment, In Everything You Do

A monk once said to me, "Take joy, Ron, in each moment, in everything you do."

In our culture, we are programmed to seek out things to do that will be fun. Whether it's going out and buying something, going to some cultural event, taking a trip, or countless other options. The point is, to do something other than what we are currently doing, something that is not required of us or part of our daily routine.

We always want something different, something new, to stimulate us. The result is that we take little or no joy in the everyday aspects of our lives. How sad when right before our eyes, every moment of every day, there is something to take joy in and value. It's all a matter of perspective.

For years I paid no attention to the monk's simple teaching and my life was very unsettled despite a disciplined practice of daily meditation. Then one day while I was meditating, this teaching came to mind and I let it sit there while I observed it and took its measure. It was one of those "eureka" moments. I resolved from that day onward, at first purposefully, to do as the monk had taught.

To take joy in each moment, one must first be present in the moment. If your thinking about this and that ... what you're going to be doing later in the day, how some problem will resolve itself, whatever ... then you can't take joy in the moment because that requires the focus of being present. There's a time for those thoughts, but it's not when you're getting dressed or doing laundry; it's when you sit down purposefully to think about those things because you need to be present for those thoughts as well.

I remember that first day well. Purposefully, I was present in each moment, something that was surprisingly rare for me despite my years of practice and meditation; such is the power of our mind. Everything I did, from the most mundane tasks of washing and drying the dishes or feeling the soft material of a knit top as I pulled it on to more mentally challenging tasks such as reading to just looking out and seeing the wind play with the grasses, tossing their seed heads this way and that in an undulating ballet ... I literally took joy in every moment, in everything I did.

This practice is only possible when we are at least aware of the negative labels ... like boring ... that we automatically apply to what we do and the world around us. Otherwise the feeling of boredom, for example, will counter any effort to find joy. Just being aware of the labels and choosing to see what else is there makes a big difference. Then you will, for example, be able to see the gray, rainy day for the wonderful, complex, interesting day that it is rather than just a "gloomy" or "ugly" day.

Whether you live in the country or the city, are rich or poor, are educated or not, this practice is available to all. When you are doing a task, even a very repetitive or menial one, or just being, you have a choice whether to be bored or take joy.

Be aware of the motions of your body or the actions of your mind in accomplishing that task and strive to do the best you can in accomplishing it. Do it purposefully, not carelessly; give it thought, give it structure, give it dignity. Be aware of the layers of texture and the countless minute miracles of nature or science that are involved in your being able to accomplish the task well or just in your being alive.

No task is mindless; no moment is without wonder and dignity.

When you are out and about, whether walking down a crowded city street or walking through a country meadow, let all your senses be alive with the experience, free of thought. Let's say you're walking in the city. You have a choice whether to focus on the dirt and noise and traffic and find it depressing, or feel the energy, the diversity of people, the amazing fact that somehow all of this works in unison. Likewise if you're walking in the country on a very hot summer day, you have the choice to focus on how uncomfortable you feel because of the heat or you can focus on the hugely varied texture and miracle of nature that is available to your senses.

This practice can be thought of as a further step in the practice of smiling mindfully. When we begin that practice and think of the wonderful things in our life, we typically think of larger, more significant things that play a major role in our lives. In this practice, we realize that all the minutiae of our lives are full of wonder and available to take joy in; we are aware of the dignity of our lives. And being present provides the access, the door to experiencing that joy and dignity.

Accepting Ourselves – Cultivating a Compassionate Heart

For years I wandered through my life frustrated. It didn't matter whether I was doing something I enjoyed or whether I was keeping up with what was happening in the world. What I enjoyed awakened cravings that left me anxious and frustrated. What disturbed me in the world left me feeling angry and agitated. And of course not having what I wanted left me frustrated. The problem was that I was approaching everything in my life from a place that lacked equanimity.

If we want to be in this world and not be agitated by all the terrible things that are happening, if we want to do the things we enjoy and give our life purpose without awakening cravings and frustration, if we want to feel at peace and content, there is one clear answer … acceptance. Until I truly accepted myself and my life as it was right then and accepted the world as it was right then, I was constantly subject to the agony caused by craving, frustration, and anger. And as will be discussed later, if you are experiencing these emotions, your child … both while in the womb and afterwards … will suffer from their impact.

The first step is to accept *ourselves* … to have compassion for ourselves and love ourselves unconditionally. For myself, as for so many people, learning to love myself unconditionally and have compassion for myself was a real challenge.

Why is it so hard for us to have compassion for ourselves? One would think that compassion would be a significant coping mechanism. But our ego, while supportive of every manner of rationalization to justify our actions or our failure to act, does not allow us to feel compassion and unconditional love for ourselves because that would undermine the power of the learned labels that it ruthlessly applies to us.

"Wait," you say, "I have felt pity towards myself or sorrow at my condition." But pity and sorrow are not compassion, at least not in the Buddhist sense. Because pity and sorrow do not negate the underlying condition as perceived by our ego. It does not change the perception that we are bad or a failure or whatever.

"Well, what about all the people out there with huge egos? Are you saying they don't love themselves?" They may love themselves, but certainly not unconditionally and they don't have compassion for themselves. People with huge egos have been shown to be at bottom very insecure people. The huge ego is a façade that hides their insecurity.

For a Buddhist (I can't speak to the other religions), the origin of compassion is love, whether for oneself or others. It is selfless and unconditional. When compassion flows from unconditional love, we do not judge ourselves anymore. We accept ourselves for what we are … without labels.

So how do we cultivate unconditional love and compassion while in the throes of our ego and learned experience? The answer comes in two parts … one organic, one intellectual.

What Buddhists call "samsara" … the particular combination of cravings and neuroses that we suffer from … is the result of our learned experience. Our self-image is actually a reflection of the image others have had of us, not a reflection of unfiltered reality … for example, we may not make much money or have much, but we are not the "failure" that we may be labeled and that we label ourselves; we may be gay, but we're not "weird" or "sick;" we may be overweight, but we are not "fat;" we may have plain looks, but we're not "homely;" those are labels set by our culture, our peers, or our family. Even fear, guilt, and shame are learned as children. All our thoughts are molded by our learned experience.

We are products of our environment and upbringing, and the way we are programmed by those factors limits in a very practical way the choices our mind can make. When you understand that, you become aware of the limited control we have over our lives when we may have thought we were quite in control of things. For all the talk of free will, its range is very restricted.

This awareness allows us to challenge the thoughts we've had about ourselves through the organic process of affirmations. Affirmations are designed to displace our negative learned feelings and labels with positive ones that reflect our true inner being.[7]

Obviously the very fact that one needs to recite affirmations, at least in the beginning, indicates that part of you doesn't really believe them. In order not to get caught in that trap … that is, affirming what you don't believe and thus perversely reinforcing that disbelief … it is of critical importance that part of you *does* believe what you are affirming and that you acknowledge at least intellectually that all the thoughts you have about yourself are labels that reflect the judgment of family or culture, they do not reflect the real you. It is important that part of you can honestly say, "yes," to each of your affirmations and that you vocalize them with conviction.

In essence, what you are doing with affirmations is having an intervention with your ego. You are telling your ego that you are going to pursue a path of peace and contentment and that you will not be deflected from this path with negative feelings. While doing this, always have compassion for your ego for it is part of you. The point is to empower yourself to follow the path you have chosen and that your heart knows is right by freeing yourself from your negative thoughts.

Recognizing the power of my ego and the entrenched nature of these negative feelings, I began many years ago reciting affirmations. At first, I recited them while giving myself a bear-hug, which I found very powerful and cathartic. Later I began reciting affirmations each morning while doing my walking meditation prior to sitting.

---

[7] Here I must digress for a moment to discuss a significant difference between the Buddhist and Christian perspective. The Buddha taught that we are all born essentially perfect. In Christianity, you have the concept of original sin and the belief that we are all born sinners who need to be saved. The psychological impact of this difference when it comes to how we view ourselves and others is substantial.

Here are some examples of affirmations that either I have used or have given to others to use. What's important is that you write affirmations for yourself that counter feelings of inadequacy or insecurity that impact you.

> *I, Ron, love, respect, and accept myself unconditionally.*
> *YES, I love myself no matter what I do or have done, what I say or have said, what I possess, who I am with, whether I am alone, whether I am acknowledged or not, whether I work — no matter what, I love and respect myself unconditionally and have compassion for myself.*

> *I, Ron, am a good person.*

> *I, Ron, am loved, valued, and needed by others. My existence makes a difference in this world.*

> *My feelings of inadequacy or failure reflect cultural or family judgments. They have no intrinsic existence; they are mere labels that are a product of my mind.*

> *My inner being is always at peace and happy even when something happens to disturb me, just like the sun is always shining and the sky is always blue even when it is cloudy.*

I continue to recite affirmations to this day. Even though my affirmations now do reflect my unequivocal, honest awareness about myself, one must be ever vigilant and aware that negative feelings may still occasionally arise even after years of practice, especially in a moment of weakness.

Another organic approach to cultivating unconditional love and compassion for oneself is to follow the instructions of Sogyal Rinpoche[8] and first "unseal the spring of loving kindness" towards yourself and then practice "tonglen" on yourself ... the Tibetan practice of taking on the suffering and pain of others and giving them your happiness, well-being, and peace of mind.

Sogyal Rinpoche recommends starting this practice by first doing it for yourself. Before one can have such compassion for others, one has to have compassion for oneself. The first step is to *"unseal the spring of loving kindness."* To do that he suggests going back in your mind and recreate, almost visualize, a love that someone gave you that really moved you. My mind wandered through several possibilities both in my adult life and childhood, when suddenly I remembered an instance with my father that was repeated often when I was small ... my father would come to my bed at night when he would get home and play with my toes.

When I remembered that episode, which had long since been forgotten, I cried because of the love that I was feeling from my father and almost simultaneously a big smile formed on my face. Rinpoche says that, *"You will remember then that even though you may not always feel that you have been loved enough, you were loved genuinely once. Knowing that now will make you feel again that you are, as that person made you feel then, worthy of love and really lovable."* And so it did.

Under his further instruction, I let my heart open and the love that flowed from it was extended to my father, to my family and friends, and to all people. I visualized holding my father as he was dying (I was not there in fact) and saying to him, "You can let go now for I know that you love me and I love you ... I will be ok." I was now ready to practice tonglen on myself.

---

[8] Sogyal Rinpoche is a highly respected Tibetan Buddhist monk and the author of *The Tibetan Book of Living and Dying,* Harper Collins, 1994.. My discussion of tonglen is taken from that book.

Rinpoche suggests, for the purpose of this exercise, dividing yourself into two aspects ... one is the aspect of you that is whole, compassionate, etc., the other is the aspect of you that has been hurt, that feels misunderstood, bitter or angry, "*who might have been unjustly treated or abused as a child, or has suffered in relationships or been wronged by society.*" As you breathe in, the first aspect opens its heart completely and receives all of the other aspect's pain and suffering. As you breathe out, the first aspect gives the other aspect all its healing love, warmth, trust, and happiness. In response, the other aspect opens its heart to this love and all pain and suffering melt away in this embrace.

What could be more appropriate for me given my history, I thought! And so, I practiced tonglen on myself with beneficial results. Indeed, as the weeks and months passed, I continued to practice both the visualization of my father's love, as well as tonglen on myself, on a regular basis. Each time I did, I felt that smile ... the smile of happiness and love ... form naturally and for many weeks tears would roll down my cheek. Clearly, this was a very cathartic experience for me.

Our awareness of the truths of samsara also opens the intellectual door to feeling compassion and respect for ourselves. For the first time in our lives, when our ego throws negative words at us ... bad, stupid, unattractive, failure ... we understand that these are words that reflect the judgment of family, peers, or our culture – they do not reflect the real us.

And although I am responsible for my life, at a deeper level I understood that until I broke out of this cycle, my ability to choose or reject and to see clearly was a limited one. Free will is in reality not free at all. Whatever we have done that we may feel remorse or regret for, those are things that often were not really within our control to do much otherwise. And so, we come to have the awareness that allows us to have compassion for ourselves, to love ourselves unconditionally.

But compassion does not stop with ourselves. Whether you believe that we are all children of God or whether you believe that we all have the true Buddha nature inside us, all mankind in every corner of the earth, regardless how poor or how rich, regardless whether kind or cruel, regardless whether civilized or not, suffers from samsara. The details may be different in different people, but the experience of samsara is universal.

The awareness of the oneness of all humanity in both its essential purity and its suffering opens the door to having compassion for all people. Even the Rwandan who wielded a machete or the Nazi SS guard who sent thousands to their death or the Charles Mansons of the world … all of these individuals are deserving of compassion because they are victims of their own samsara. Regarding all one can truly say, "there but for the grace of God go I."[9]

Accepting Life

How do we find acceptance for our life, when we've spent our life not accepting it?

Even when in the grip of cravings and frustrations, we are still usually capable in calmer moments of being aware of the wonderful things in our life … be it our family, our job, our hobbies, our friends, the wonders of nature, the warmth of our bed, things large and small, whatever. I don't mean to be glib, but regardless how dissatisfied one is with ones life, there are always aspects that give us joy or that we feel good about when we stop and think about it. That certainly was true for me.

Is there a way of using that awareness to make progress on the path to accepting life? I believe the answer is, yes.

---

[9] Jesus' statement from the cross is also very relevant, "Father forgive them for they know not what they do."

The first step I took was to work with this revealed fact. I focused on the good things in my life without saying, "Yes, but I don't have … . " I tried to be aware of those things and be grateful for them throughout the day, especially when I got up in the morning and when I went to bed at night. This is the teaching contained in the previous sections on "Smiling Mindfully" and "Taking Joy in Each Moment."

When you have, if not turned your mind from your cravings, at least given the good things in your life equal time in your mind, then you are ready for the second step … understanding the difference between skillful and unskillful desires.

One reason why we have a problem with acceptance is our fear of the unknown. "How will I pursue my life if I accept things as they are now?" Even if we understand that acceptance does not mean resignation, we think that acceptance entails letting go of our hopes and dreams. And the idea of that is unacceptable.

But that is not the case. Acceptance does not mean letting go of all desires and hopes … just unskillful ones. What turns an otherwise skillful desire into an unskillful one is often its origin in a lack of equanimity. If it is based on your running from what is, if you are dissatisfied, then it becomes unskillful; it becomes a craving.

And what causes this lack of equanimity? Why do these hopes and dreams seem so crucial to our being that they create the destructive cravings that bring us only pain and frustration?

Hopes and dreams may be a function of human nature, but the lack of equanimity that transforms them into powerful cravings that cause suffering is caused by something else … a lack of acceptance of ourselves, of who we are, and a lack of acceptance of our lives. If we do not have compassion for ourselves and love ourselves *unconditionally*, if we want to be something or someone other,

29

we cannot accept our lives and will suffer. If we are so blinded by cravings that we cannot see that we have what we need, what is most important to us,[10] right now, we cannot accept our lives and we will suffer. To break this pattern and find equanimity, we have only to be present, focus on what we "have" right now that brings us joy and learn to loves ourselves unconditionally.

So, if following the guidance of the previous subsection we have accepted ourselves, if we love ourselves unconditionally and have compassion for ourselves, then we are almost there; our equanimity has begun to blossom. If we just accept our life as it is right now, our equanimity will be complete and our skillful desires will remain skillful; our cravings and frustration will cease.

Another answer to this barrier lies in the teaching, "it's just the way it is." Once many years ago, I asked a monk why, if we are all born essentially perfect, suffering was such a common human experience. His answer was, "It's just the way it is. It's like the law of thermodynamics."

When I heard his words it was like a huge burden was lifted from my shoulders. While acceptance was still key to achieving peace and serenity, that acceptance was made easier by understanding that things are the way they are because it's just the way they are … even if something still did have a negative label in my mind. It wasn't really for me to accept; it just was. Similarly, the age-old question, "Why me?" misses the point … it has nothing to do with "me." Having absorbed the teaching of "it's just the way it is," it

---

[10] And by "what we need" and "important" I don't just mean the specific things we have at the moment, realizing that all things are impermanent, but the awareness that at any moment of any day of any year, there are things we experience that will bring us well-bring and joy … whether they be things outside or inside of ourselves. Even in our darkest moments when our world may look very bleak, we know that those strengthening experiences are open to us if we are open to them.

was easier for me to accept my life and the world around me.

Once I understood these things and that acceptance does not mean consigning myself to a life in the future that is devoid of hopes and desires, then I was able to take the third step, which is to *truly* accept … happily … my life as being the way it is right now. These concepts are synergistic. This is not a mental trick; it is an honest way of resolving a very real obstacle to finding peace and happiness.

The change this brought about in my life cannot be overstated. As an example, for most of my life, I did not love myself unconditionally or have compassion for myself. And so I was obsessed with finding companionship, both for security and to feel wanted or loved. The perfectly healthy and skillful desire for friends or loved ones was transformed into a deep craving and frustration. My insecurity and anxiety were so extreme that even when I was in a relationship, I would be so afraid of losing it that my craving and frustration would continue unabated.

But once I began to love myself unconditionally and have compassion, and began to accept my life as it was, knowing that I could still have skillful hopes and dreams, my demons deflated and my desire for companionship returned to its skillful state. I know now that my fear of being alone was just a function of the negative view I had of myself based on learned experience. There is no fear of being alone when you love yourself unconditionally and are at one with all things.

But beware, the line separating skillful and unskillful desires is very thin. Desires have a way of pulling one away from ones acceptance. In order to keep our desires skillful, we must thus be disciplined in the practice of gratitude and acceptance until that is so deeply engrained that they become a paradigm of our life.

One also needs to be aware that because our ego and its cravings are so strong and wily, it is quite possible that when one reads these sections and responds positively to accepting oneself and ones life as it is, that acceptance will be merely an illusion, a self-deception. In that case, nothing will have changed and your cravings will be as strong and destructive as before. That is why I italicized the word "truly" when I wrote, "to *truly* accept my life."

What one needs to do in order to not fall into this trap is to give your acceptance some space and time to take root. This is after all a major shift for us after spending most of our lives not accepting. And we need to recognize that our craving for things is basically an addiction ... we feel we need them to be happy ... and so it is helpful to follow the practice of 12-step programs and commit to not entertaining any of our desires/cravings for a period of time ... however long it takes until you can honestly say that you accept yourself and your life as it is right now.

Your ego will certainly scream at you, "But I want [whatever]!" When it does that, you need to respond that you have what you need right now and you have faith that if you live each day with equanimity, the future will take care of itself. End of story!

As regards accepting the state of the world as it is right now, my compassion for all beings together with the teaching of "it's just the way it is" has altered the nature of my interaction with the news of the day and the world at large. No longer do I become angry and agitated. Instead I have concern and compassion.

As you focus on the wonderful things in your life and begin developing unconditional love and compassion for yourself and others, accepting your life as it is now, and freeing yourself from unskillful desires, then you will begin to experience the peace, contentment, and happiness that provides the clarity necessary to exercise your best judgment in all areas of your life, both for your benefit as well as your child's.

Staying Grounded

Once I achieved a platform of peace and happiness, the challenge was then to maintain it. In addition to continuing doing the things that brought me this peace, there was one more necessary element ... staying grounded.

As I make my way through life, there were and will likely continue to be many challenges to my peace and happiness. I have found that this is especially true of anything that I put energy and effort into.

Even if we truly accept our life as it is, when we put effort into an activity, our ego often arises, looking to be stroked. And if it is not stroked, we get frustrated. Since putting forth effort is an integral part of living, is there an answer to this conundrum?

Your initial reaction may be ... "Ah, this is a sign that I've been deceiving myself; I'm not truly accepting of my life." While that may of course be true, it is not necessarily so.

It is an inherent part of human nature that when we put forth effort, we do it for a reason, for an end ... for example, to help others, to further our career, to resolve a problem, or just to learn or create something ... otherwise we would not put forth the effort to begin with. (NOTE: If you are doing such an activity because you feel the need to fix an inadequacy you feel, to "improve" yourself, then the activity is not skillful because it stems from a lack of equanimity that needs to be addressed.) Even if we truly accept our life, our ego often attaches unseen to such effort. And so if there's a setback, even if we are present, we will be frustrated rather than saying, "it's just the way it is."

For those efforts where, once we have produced something, we are dependent on others for its acceptance/use, a different dynamic often occurs. Rather than letting it go at that point, not thinking about the future, we often find ourselves consumed by doubt and desire during the seemingly eternal process of waiting for feedback and check our email or phone messages constantly for some word. This is very demoralizing and robs us of our peace. Without question, our ego has attached to the effort.

The solution to this inescapable conundrum is to stay grounded. Whether it's your job, your volunteer work, or a book you're trying to write or market, you must make sure that the task does not consume you and rob you of your peace.

We can stay grounded by keeping the activity in perspective, which requires first being present, which will allow us to be aware of the things and people that bring us joy, know that we have what we need, what is important to us, right now, maintain our focus in life on those things, and be disciplined in our practice of acceptance, loving ourselves unconditionally. Meditation is also very helpful.

The key is to see your frustration or anger as a red flag … it is your canary in a mine … that one of two things is happening: either you are engaged in an activity or pursuing a goal which is not healthy for you or the activity or goal is in the abstract a healthy one, but you are approaching it in an unhealthy way, for example it has become a craving that stems from a lack of equanimity.

When you experience frustration or anger, the first thing you must do is stop. Without stopping you cannot apply your spirituality to the situation. Center yourself by watching your breathing; one method is to simply say, "Breathing in, I'm aware I'm breathing in; breathing out, I'm aware I'm breathing out."

First determine whether the activity is unhealthy … is it something that will harm others or yourself. If not, then determine whether it's just an ego trip. Ask, "Could this effort realistically make a difference?" The more macro the effort, the more likely that the answer to this question may be a painful, no. If it is either harmful or just an extension of your ego, then you need to drop the project to regain your sense of peace and contentment.

But if your effort really could make a difference, whether in one person's life or many, but the problem is that you are approaching it from a lack of equanimity, despite your general acceptance of your life, then you need to find a way to approach the activity in a healthy, non-craving way.

For most types of efforts you will help yourself stay grounded by limiting your time exposure to the activity. Keep your commitment appropriate with your focus on the things that bring you joy, that give you strength, and thus limit any potential negative impact.

You can't do that with your job, of course. Especially in today's work environment when there is often pressure to work almost 24/7. But even here, you must not only carve out time for your family and other things that bring you joy ... those things must psychologically be the center of your life, not your work. It is a sad statement of our culture that for many people work has become their life; they live to work, not work to live.

A helpful compliment to maintaining the right focus in your life is to remember the teaching ... it's just the way it is. Whatever is bothering you about the effort you are making, it's just the way it is.

It's also helpful to remember that we have no control over the future and can have no idea what is going to transpire ... therefore why obsess about what will happen? It's a no-win situation that robs you of your peace in the present, which is where you really need it. Instead, have faith that if you live each day well with equanimity, the future will take care of itself ... although not necessarily in the way you have planned.

Another tool that helps keep things in perspective is to engage in activities that relax you, calm you (beyond the spiritual ones already noted in this chapter). As adults, most of us have a real deficit in this area. Even activities that we supposedly do to relax us, to get away from things … like playing golf, playing an instrument, shopping, whatever … do not relax us because our ego is involved in those activities. They may be a distraction, but they are not calming.

What you need to do is some activity that puts you in touch with your inner child, that innocent being who was and is still free from the burdens of life and most learned experience. Most adults in our culture are closed off to their inner child; somehow it's not felt appropriate for adults to engage in childlike behavior or activities. And yet those activities, and the simple laughter that often accompanies them, give one access to the well of innocent joy that only a child experiences. Whether you used to love coloring books, climbing trees, playing with your dog (this is not to be confused with what adults do with their dogs in a dog park), or whatever, allow yourself the simple joy of immersing yourself in such activities with some regularity.

There is a deeper answer, however, to the question of how to stay grounded. There is a line in the classic Chinese poem, *Affirming Faith in Mind*, that says, "When the mind rests undisturbed then nothing in the world offends. And when no thing can give offense, then all obstructions cease to be."[11]

We are frustrated in these situations because our ego takes offense when we are not stroked. And the ego takes offense because these situations disturb our mind and our ego arises.

Why do these situations disturb our mind? Because we do not experience them free of labels, free of our past. For most of us these situations touch the deepest insecurities from our childhood about who we are, how we are valued, and whether we are liked or loved. Whenever we put

---

[11] Roshi Phillip Kapleau, *Chants*, Rochester Zen Center, 1990

ourselves, our talent, our credibility on the line, this ego insecurity is awakened.

And so the deeper, more fundamental, solution to such frustration is to explore the truth, through meditation or quiet thought, that fear, guilt, and shame are learned. We must free ourselves from the past. Whatever made us feel insecure as children, that emotional reaction was a learned experience and does not reflect who we really were; it was a cultural or family judgment. And those judgments do not speak the truth; they are biased. Our cultural obsession with "improving" ourselves is not founded on a desire to learn more or do other things, it is based on a perception that we are inadequate in some way, that we are failures, and that that needs to be fixed. But we are not inadequate; we are not failures. These perceptions of ours are learned.

And so, being aware of the nature of these perceptions, we begin to be able to experience ourselves without any labels. And we are better able to love ourselves unconditionally.

For the Sake of Your Child and Yourself

This is all probably much more than you bargained for when you picked up this book. But if you really want to raise a happy child, and the basic points I make about our lives ring true to you, then there really is no option but to first detox yourself, as it were, by taking the steps I've suggested. It will take a lot of patience and discipline, but persevere with a joyful spirit for the ultimate benefit to you, your child, all those you hold dear, and all those with whom you come into contact will be beyond measure.

Chapter 3
During Pregnancy

The basic fact that informs this chapter is that you and your baby are biologically one in the sense that your blood flows through it and is its sole source of nourishment and life. Anything that effects your blood thus effects your baby's blood, and since your baby is in the stage of development, the impact of those changes in the blood can be far more potent on your baby than on you.

You are probably familiar with the warnings that smoking cigarettes, or drinking, or taking recreational drugs, or eating fish taken from PCB contaminated water can be harmful to the baby in your womb. Again the reason is that the harmful ingredients of these products get into the baby through the common bloodstream.

What is, however, not commonly known is that a mother's emotions impact the developing baby. Recent studies suggest that, "stress in the womb can affect a baby's temperament and neurobehavioral development. Infants whose mothers experienced high levels of stress while pregnant, particularly in the first trimester, show signs of more depression and irritability. 'Who you are and what you're like when you are pregnant will affect who that baby is,' says Janet DiPietro, a developmental psychologist at Johns Hopkins University. 'Women's psychological functioning during pregnancy – their anxiety level, stress, personality -- ultimately affects the temperament of their babies. It has to ... the baby is awash in all the chemicals produced by the mom.'"[12]

---

[12] http://www.medicinenet.com/script/main/art.asp?articlekey=51730&page=2

This research shows the importance of a happy and content, loving mother to the future psychological welfare of her child. But the state of the father during this period is just as important, for if the father is stressed out, anxious, angry, etc., those emotions will most likely impact the mother and through the mother, the baby.

Understanding this basic fact places a new responsibility on both parents during pregnancy. And underscores why the points made in the previous chapter are so critical to raising a happy child.

Please note, you cannot achieve the desired effect by repressing your anger or stress because that process does not eliminate the stress, and in many ways just makes it worse. Instead, you must find a way to, if not end, greatly reduce your stress and anxiety through the processes that were suggested.

Having a baby is a momentous responsibility. And it starts not at birth, nor even at conception, but in the years before conception, for turning yourself and your husband into reasonably happy and secure persons in the face of all that you've experienced at the hands of family, peers, and the larger culture is not a short-term project.

Now, don't respond to this statement by throwing up your hands in frustration. Keep in mind that every bit of improvement in your psychological functioning will help your child. Even if you do not achieve the level of peace and contentment that is possible, any step in that direction will be of benefit.

And even if you're reading this book when you're already pregnant, or after your child is born, following the process laid out in the first chapter will still have great benefit. This is one of those instances where one can truly say, "better late than never."

Chapter 4
Who Is Your Baby?

For the reasons indicated in the previous chapter, your baby comes into the world with a temperament that has been formed during its time in the womb. But regardless what a baby's temperament is … even if it's anxious or angry … the type of person your baby develops into is primarily the result of the environment that you provide it; the nurturing, support, and love that you give or don't give your child. As well as, of course, intellectual stimulation.

Contrary to the teaching of some religions, we are not all born sinners. No baby carries that burden when he is born. That is instead something that is thrust upon him by his society. If a child is told he is bad, he will indeed become bad. If a child has a difficult temperament and is treated like a bad child, rather than being treated with loving affection, then that child will become bad. These are self-fulfilling prophecies.

It is not the child that is bad or stupid or whatever pejorative that may be applied; it is the parents' treatment of the child and their reaction to its temperament that causes this development. Which in turn is often a function of their own anxieties, stress, and insecurity, which hopefully the lessons of this book will diminish.

In short, your baby is pretty much a blank slate. It has its temperament. And it has its genetic pre-dispositions. But of far greater impact is the home that you provide your child. You have the ability to make the difference between a child being happy or sad, confident or insecure, productive or unproductive, angry or content.

Yes, the culture we live in will have a huge impact on your child. But how he reacts to that culture, how he navigates its stresses and expectations, will be a function of the character that results from the way in which you raise him and the guidance you provide along the way..

Please note that I am not saying here that if, for example, you raise your child within a strict moral structure that he will end up having a strong moral sense. If that moral structure is divorced from an atmosphere of loving kindness, then the child is far more likely to rebel against the structure provided by the parent then accept it. (For more on this dynamic, see the following chapters.)

Bottom line ... who your baby is, and the child and adult your baby becomes, is a function of your actions. Much of what parents do that in subtle or not so subtle ways harms their children is done unwittingly, certainly with no ill will. That may spare the parent a sense of guilt, but it does not alter the fact that the parent has harmed the child.

The object of this book is to enlighten parents so that they understand both their own dynamics and that of their child so that both parents and child grow into happy and content people.

Chapter 5
The First Months and Years

There are three inter-related principles that should guide all your interactions with your child at all stages of its development…show your child unconditional love and compassion, listen to your child deeply, and speak to your child with loving kindness. A fourth principle is essential to the implementation of these three … consistency. These principles may sound like a no-brainer, but sadly this is not the case.

In case you read this as sounding like I am advising you to spoil your child, give in to its every whim, as you will see in this chapter and in the following ones, following these principles does *not* mean giving your child whatever it wants whenever it wants it. Such action is neither an expression of unconditional love nor helpful to your child developing into a happy child and adult.

If you look around you or think about your own childhood you will find that these principles are violated more than they are followed. In this and the following chapters, I discuss the import of these principles at different critical stages of your child's development and provide practical examples both of how to and how not to interact with your child.

Research has shown consistently that the first months and years of a child's life are the most critical period for developing a sense of security and a healthy emotional psyche. This is sometimes referred to as the bonding period, but the impact goes far beyond child-parent relationships.

The primary nurturing agent during this period is, not surprisingly, the mother. Though the father is important here too, as are siblings. Deprived of the necessary nurturing contact, a child is subject, depending on the extent of deprivation, to develop negative psychosocial traits as it matures such as delinquency, increased aggression, and depression.

A child signals that it needs nurturing contact in a variety of easily recognizable ways … crying, smiling, and locomotion, for example. Most people's natural instinct is to respond to such displays by a baby in the desired way, by picking it up and holding it, showing it affection. This is showing your child unconditional love and compassion at this stage of its life.

There is probably no baby that gets none of this desired nurturing contact and most get quite a good bit of it. But it is also true that there are few babies who receive this nurturing when desired consistently. Whether it's just letting the baby cry … either because it's inconvenient just then to tend to the baby or they subscribe to the theory that crying makes the baby stronger … or scolding or even yelling at a baby for crying (this is obviously not listening or speaking with loving kindness) or ignoring its smiling or locomotion as being cute but not requiring any action by the mother or other caregiver, a baby's call for nurturing often goes unanswered.

Sometimes I've witnessed situations where it almost seems that parents feel that a baby makes a reasoned choice to cry and if they feel the crying is unreasonable, they just ignore it. A baby's cry, however, is not reasoned but instinctive, and if not responded to, the reaction will likewise be instinctive.

A recent article in *The New Yorker*[13] noted approvingly that the French don't worry that frustrating their children will damage them … they think it will help them...including routinely letting a baby cry for five minutes before picking it up.[14] For the reason just noted, I think one has to

---

[13] Elizabeth Kolbert, "Spoiled Rotten," *The New Yorker*, July 2, 2012, p.76

[14] Dr. Harvey Karp's *The Happiest Baby on the Block*, Bantam, 2003, in addition to providing excellent examples of how to provide nurturing to

differentiate between an infant and a toddler, and between "frustrating" a child and teaching it at an appropriate age that even though one is loved unconditionally, one can't always get what one wants.

Because an infant's cry is instinctive, not reasoned, one must respond promptly to provide the nurturing it needs at that stage. Dealing with a toddler is another matter. If you've developed a loving relationship with your child, your toddler will not be frustrated when you explain the facts of life; your toddler will understand that he or she is loved unconditionally even though they aren't being given what they want. Learning not to get frustrated is a much better lesson if a child and adult is to be happy than learning how to cope with frustration.

As a child starts to crawl and walk, there are many more occasions where a child may do something that upsets a parent under some stress, which results in the child getting scolded ... "bad boy" ... or yelled at. Such a reaction by the parent signals the child that the parent's love is conditional and that confuses the child.

It is clearly important that a child, as soon as it is capable of understanding *and* responding, learn the rules of how one navigates life, in ways both large and small. But the way for a parent to explain the rules to a child is quietly and with compassion, not to yell or scold.[15]

---

your baby when it cries that mimics what it received in the womb, his "Cuddle Cure," slams this concern about spoiling a baby by equating a baby's first 3 months to a fourth trimester. You cannot hold your baby enough, he says; the need is that great.

[15] As Dr. Karp puts it, the parent needs to build a great relationship with a toddler by using respectful words and setting clear limits, not yelling or scolding or being a buddy. *The Happiest Toddler on the Block,* Bantam, 2005. This works because it is how you apply deep listening and speaking with loving kindness to a toddler. Even his "Fast-Food Rule" falls under this principle. Indeed, most of the techniques in Dr. Karp's popular *Happiest* books are examples of the overarching principles that I posit apply to all stages of a child's development.

Which brings up another interrelated principle in raising a happy child … whenever criticism is given, it should be given in a way that is compassionate and shows unconditional love and loving kindness. So for example, while it's important for a child to understand the word,"no," the tone of voice you use when saying, "no," makes the difference between compassionate discipline and angry discipline. On the other hand, it is important for "no" to mean just that, rather than something a child can get around.

Why do so many parents not follow these simple rules, or not follow them consistently? For contemporary parents the answers, regardless of socioeconomic status, often revolve around stress. The source of stress may be very different depending on ones life circumstances, but the result is the same.

Additionally, the needs of a baby or young child are sadly often viewed by a parent as inconvenient or annoying, not because of some particular stress but because of the parent's preoccupation with itself and its own agenda. The parent is busily occupied with whatever the parent is doing at the moment.

But in conceiving and giving birth to a child, you as parent have undertaken a serious responsibility. A baby, and even a young child, is a very fragile being. You are the world to your child. It looks to you for everything, certainly for nourishing love and affection and security. While your child is growing up, there can be no excuse for depriving it of the emotional nourishment it needs to develop into a happy, confident, secure person.

If you reflect on your own childhood, those of your friends, and the parent/child interactions you see around you, you will find ample evidence of parent behavior that is the opposite of unconditional love, compassion, and speaking with loving kindness. Too many parents say that that's the way they were raised and they survived; besides, it's a rough world out there, can't have a thin skin. While that may be true, they survived as unhappy, insecure persons, and no parent should want to either intentionally or unwittingly inflict such similar damage on its child.

One important rule about navigating life that a child should start learning early on is how to interact with other people. This often comes up with toddlers when parents try to get them to play nicely with others. Typically, you might hear a parent tell a child that the child ought to share or not to hit or counter whatever socially negative or embarrassing attitude the child is displaying.

But such comments are made in a vacuum and rarely make an impact on the child. Instead, you need to explain to your child that just like you interact with each other with loving kindness and all that entails, he or she should interact with playmates and others in the same way. Even if someone is mean to your child, your child should not be mean in response. (Defending oneself from being hit is another matter.) Children should be encouraged at the earliest possible age to act towards others as they would like others to act towards them and to view all people as part of a large human family.

A common issue that impacts the need for your child to be nurtured is the working mother. Obviously, when the mother is away at work, she cannot be there for her child. Ideally, all mothers would be at home with their child until the child goes to school, but that is not a realistic expectation in today's world.

But although that financial imperative is often inescapable, you should stop and think and discuss with your spouse/significant other how critical it really is. Since you're reading this book, you will understand that there's a difference between being able to keep food on the table and a roof over your head, and being able to afford discretionary niceties or maintain your career. When you balance the welfare of your child with bringing in more money or maintaining your career trajectory, which is of greater importance? At difficult moments like this, always remember that having a child was a choice you made; your child had no say whether to be born or not.

If both parents working is indeed necessary, then it is of critical importance that another nurturing caregiver … whether it's a grandmother, a nanny, or someone else … be there to meet the child's needs on a consistent basis, and that they be provided with an understanding of what that entails. A day care center, regardless how professional, will typically not provide the level of emotional nurturing a child needs.

By reading this book, you have shown that you desire to be a caring, loving parent. If you work at it, that is certainly within your ability.

Chapter 6
Childhood – The Grade School Years

When a child enters grade school, while the critical nurturing period is past, the parenting role becomes in many ways even more important and difficult because your child is now entering a phase where his mind is more active and he is being exposed more to the expectations and pressures of the culture around him. If going from the womb to life is a shock to a child, going from the safe and supportive (hopefully) confines of the home to the wild world of school and the broader culture is often equally stressful to the child.

Whether your child is a boy or a girl, the importance of unconditional love, compassion, deep listening and speaking with loving kindness … and consistency … is not lessened during this phase of their life. While they may seem at times like little grown-ups and quite precocious, they are still children. They are still fragile and they need nurturing and love … and direction … to develop into healthy, happy adults.

In this chapter, I will deal with several issues that you will without question confront during this period … tension in the family, peer pressure, the lure of technology, building self-confidence, and working parents.

The Family

There will always be a certain amount of tension between parents and children and sibling rivalry … that's just a function of our biological and evolutionary makeup. But such tension can exist within an atmosphere of unconditional love and compassion ... the two are not mutually exclusive.

How can you as a parent foster the growth of an atmosphere of unconditional love and compassion in your home? Building on your actions during your child's early years, the most important way is by example. In your interactions with your spouse/significant other and children, always show compassion and unconditional love. An essential component of that is deep listening and loving speech.

Think about your childhood experiences or what you've observed in other families. What is missing so often within the family, and of course elsewhere, is deep listening and loving speech. How often do parents listen deeply to their children when they speak, which involves more than just hearing what they say? And do parents always speak to them with loving kindness? Hardly.

At this stage of their life, your children will come to you constantly with questions of all kinds, not just of an intellectual nature but also on matters concerning their emotional state. Or they may not bring some things up but you as parent need to know your children well enough and be observant enough that you can sense when something is bothering them and coax it out of them.

Especially when dealing with emotional issues, deep listening is critical. You need to put aside whatever is on your mind and focus on listening to your child. Truly hear and understand what they are saying and why they are saying it. Only then can you respond by speaking with loving kindness for only then will your response be meaningful and helpful rather than a toss-off.

When you have a difference of opinion or you feel your child needs direction, always do it within a loving context. The point that needs to be clearly felt by your child is that although there are differences or criticisms, they do not disturb the underlying feelings of unconditional love and compassion.

If you act consistently in this manner, it will also help you manage interaction among your children. If you happen to witness your children acting towards each other badly, you can then point to your example and explain the coexistence between rivalry or disagreement on the one hand and unconditional love and compassion on the other and the need to watch what one says.

Another way to foster such an atmosphere is to encourage activities in which family members compliment each other, acting as a community, rather than competing with each other all the time as individuals. Much has been made of the development of team spirit in the workplace. The same approach is much needed within the contemporary home. In the past when all children had their chores to do, this teamwork was taken for granted; now it is typically nonexistent.

Peer Pressure

One of the most difficult stresses facing both children and parents during this stage of their life and later is peer pressure ... the pressure of the child's peers and the broader culture to conform to its demands and expectations. And there is almost no aspect of your child's life that won't be impacted by peer pressure, so how you and your child navigate this issue is of vital importance.

If you have done a good job so far in raising your child, he or she will be secure and have good self-esteem. That will make dealing with peer pressure much easier, but it doesn't make it go away. Even if your child is well-adjusted, the desire to be part of your peer group, to conform, is huge for children. No child wants to be labeled as different.

The first thing is for you as a parent to be clear in your own mind about what areas of peer pressure are ok and which are not. For example, one major area of peer pressure is how kids dress. Except for holding a reasonable line on the expense of your child's wardrobe, what he or she chooses to wear should be left mostly up to them. It may not be your taste, but clothing is the easiest and least potentially problematic way for a child to fit into his peer group. Children need to be able to express themselves, and this is one way they do it. Besides, you know that this is an area where your child will change many times over the course of the years because the cultural dictates will change as they get older. So this is not an area where you should challenge your child, except in an extreme circumstance.

On the other hand, peer pressure to treat weak kids poorly, to make fun of certain types of people ... those kind of attitudes are things which hopefully your child will see as wrong and reject, or will come to you with a question which you can help him sort out.

What you should do when your child starts school is sit down and have a discussion about peer pressure. He needs to understand that sometimes his friends and acquaintances may have different moral standards and attitudes from his, and that it's important that he do what he thinks is right. Tell your child that you have confidence in his or her ability to know right from wrong, fair from unfair, and to act accordingly ... that you trust your child not to just go along with the crowd. But if your child ever has any questions about what's expected of him from his peers, he should be made totally comfortable coming to you to get your input.

The Lure of Technology

One area of peer or cultural pressure needs special mention. Our culture each year is becoming more and more engrossed with technology-based interaction. Whether its Facebook or Twitter or digital games, the youth of America (and for that matter much of the world) is totally absorbed in this virtual world. You as a parent have to decide just what aspects of this technology and how much of it is good for your child's development.

In case you haven't been following the flow of reports on this phenomenon, the reason why this is such an important issue for your child's current and future happiness is that studies are showing that people are replacing human contact with electronic contact, even between friends and acquaintances, with the result that while there is an illusion of being more connected and intimate with others than ever before, in fact people are less connected and more lonely. This goes beyond the much-publicized issue of why people feel compelled to disclose so much information about their private lives to hoards of basically unknown people.

This is one of those areas where it's not a question of right or wrong, good or bad. There's really nothing in your child's experience to allow him to judge whether something like this might harm him or not. So since it's certainly true that all his peers will be doing these things nonstop, he is likely to go with the flow.

It's therefore an area that requires some diplomatic intervention by you. There are some things, like time spent with video/digital games, where you may just lay down a time limit, or also some content standards. The issue of social media can be handled as one of balance. There's no reason to forbid your child to use these products ... it will be an increasingly important skill to have ... but he does need to understand that they don't take the place of one-on-one interactions with people, whether in person or on the phone. Your child needs to begin understanding that just because it's the latest technology does not mean that it's progress.

Building Self-Confidence

Given current trends in our culture, it is important to note that one does not build self-confidence, or help your children, by not offering criticism. Unconditional love does not mean uncritical love.

Giving criticism with loving kindness involves a variety of things. First, your tone of voice is very important. Never criticize in a harsh tone. Second, when you criticize your child, start by giving him positive feedback on some aspect of what he's done, so that the criticism is put in context. Third, if the criticism concerns an area of activity regarding which you have not had occasion to have a discussion with your child previously, make sure you explain where you're coming from; give your child the benefit of some back-story.

Giving praise is also not as simple as it may seem. Much has been written about how the current generation of teenagers and 20-somethings feel that they have everything coming to them and that they can do no wrong. They are accused of being intoxicated by self-esteem and parents are accused of aiding and abetting this state through a combination of unreserved praise and support and a lack of parental criticism and control.

But in a cruel irony, while a display of bravado and feelings of being special may be common, this is not due to their increase in self-esteem. On the contrary, it is yet further evidence of how insecure and hollow our children's lives have become. They are lost.

It is a well-known psychological fact that having a huge ego is typically a façade, a coping mechanism for deep feelings of insecurity and anxiety. And the size of the ego and extent of aggression is directly related to the amount of insecurity.

Many writers have noted that the generation of people now in their 20s grew up bathed in praise and messages that they are special. While it may well be that such action on the part of parents was meant to increase self-esteem, in fact it often increases insecurity. When a child is told he is special, but feels deep down that he is not because the praise is not grounded on anything specific or is just absurdly effusive, he feels he is being told that he is expected to be special and thus feels under pressure to indeed be special, creating huge insecurities. Or the child feels that words are not to be trusted, creating a feeling of cynicism and insecurity.

If children do something that warrants praise or positive notice, they should be given that feedback clearly based on specific behavior or accomplishment. Your children need to feel that you believe in them, and that belief needs to be based on something tangible. But if a child warrants criticism or disciplining, that should also be given clearly based on specific behavior and always within the context of unconditional love and compassion. The attitude, "My child right or wrong," is not helpful to your child. Above all, you as a parent or a spouse must be consistent in your interactions.

There is another caveat regarding providing helpful advice or criticism ... be sure that your actions are not an expression of your ego. If you're a worry-wort, if you are always worried about your child doing something that will harm them in some way, if you try to protect them from such problems, if you feel you need to manage their lives to insure their "success," the chances are that this is largely an expression of your ego. You want to feel that you are helpful, that you can solve problems, that you can keep your child from harms way, that you can insure their success. While this sounds like benevolent action, it is your ego working and it's not helpful.

The reality is that your child needs to find out for himself what works and what doesn't. That will undoubtedly involve some pain, because we don't always make the right decisions or are careless. But the only way to grow is to learn from mistakes, and unfortunately they usually have to be our own. The only way to gain self-confidence is to do things yourself. If your child feels that you don't have faith in their ability to tackle things themselves, that you micromanage their activity, then they will not gain that all-important self-confidence. Your lack of faith in them will become a self-fulfilling prophecy.

The line that separates helpful advice and criticism from self-confidence-robbing comments is the pattern of activity. Occasional advice or criticism if properly given as suggested above is probably not a manifestation of your ego and can indeed be helpful. However, if you find that you are constantly concerned about your child or spouse and frequently make comments, then that behavior crosses the line.

Even when making occasional comments, though, reflect on whether you are listening deeply and speaking with loving kindness, or whether you are expressing your ego. Would perhaps the kinder approach in a particular situation be to say nothing or something different?

This is an area of family interaction that is full of minefields. Don't expect perfection from yourself; undoubtedly you will make some wrong choices. But try to be as aware as possible of these issues so that for the most part you will act in what is truly the best interest of your child.

Working Parents

There seems to be a general feeling among parents that they are freed from any obligation to stay home to take care of the children once they reach school age and are gone for a good part of the day. But while that may be true for the hours that children are at school, their need for parenting the rest of the time remains undiminished. Children at this age are still quite fragile and continue to require the nourishment of loved ones.

Let me site a few personal examples. By all accounts (I have no actual memory of my early years), I was a very happy baby and child. From photos, stories, and notes in my baby book, a picture emerges of a much-loved child who was very happy, always in a good mood. But when I was 4, we moved to a different town where my father had started a new business.

The result of my father's new responsibilities was that I now rarely saw him ... only at breakfast and at weekend dinners. At all other times he was either working in the office or on the road selling.

I, being a child, did not understand why my father was no longer a large part of my daily life. And I came to the unfortunate conclusion that my father no longer loved me. This was reinforced by his newly exhibited anger at me because of my bad eating habits, which resulted in unpleasantness when I did see him.

This presumption of mine that I was no longer loved by my father, despite much evidence that he continued to care for me, caused me much grief and neurosis. For much of my life, I felt that I was undeserving of love and that love was always conditional. This resulted in various social dysfunction problems.

In another family I was friendly with in my 20s, the mother went back to work after the kids were all in school. They had an au pair to see to the children when they came home from school and the mother did not work summers when they were off. Despite that, they were clearly very upset that their mother was working and was not there for them. This exhibited itself once by the children egging each other on about how terrible their mother was. It got to such a nasty pitch that I finally slapped one of the children to stop their behavior. Again, these were much-loved children and their mother had made far more effort than most to still be there for her children, even after they entered school. But for these children that was not enough.

The last example is a positive one from my own life again. One of my most pleasant memories of childhood is coming home after school each day. I would open the front door, sing out "Yoo-hoo," and then head to the kitchen where my mother would either be ironing or cooking. As she worked, she listened to the soap operas then popular on the radio … "The Lives of Helen Trent," "Pepper Young," and "Stella Dallas" … and I would listen to those programs with her as I drank the milk and ate the piece of cake she had given me. I felt very safe in those moments.

I site these examples as proof of how important a parent's nurturing continues to be even at this stage of a child's life. And even in situations where the child is clearly shown much love. Children, being intuitive, emotional, beings without well-developed reasoning capability, often come to false conclusions about events in their life, which even though minor in the larger scope of things, can take on an outsized significance in their psychology.

If both parents must work to provide for the family, as opposed to have more discretionary money to acquire more things, which while in keeping with the consumer addiction of our culture is not really necessary, or maintaining a career, then you must be very sure that your child understands why you are not there when he gets home from school or in the summers, and make sure there is no question in your child's mind that you love him.

Chapter 7
The Teenage Years

The teenage years are of course the bane of most parent's existence. Children are experiencing changes in their hormones and all the pressure and stress that come from the demands of those hormones. And they intensely feel the need to be their own person, which often presents itself through actions which rebel against authority, especially parents.

Even in the best of situations, these times can be trying for both parents and children. But there is no question that if you have been applying the lessons of this book, you're task during these years will be much easier. The unconditional love, compassion, deep listening and speaking with loving kindness ... and consistency ... that you have shown your child will have forged a strong healthy relationship between you that will result in minimal rebellion and a more rational and healthy way of dealing with hormonal stresses.

If you are reading this book for the first time and your child is already a teenager and a handful, the lessons of this book are never ... well almost never ... too late. Regardless of the façade that teenagers construct, they are underneath it as fragile as ever, for now they are experiencing another major stress in their life ... the hormones of puberty.

All teenagers, whether they would admit it or not, or realize it or not, desperately need all the aspects of parental nurturing and love that we have been discussing in this book. They need your support to handle the psychological forces that are arraigned against them during these difficult years.

All the issues that I dealt with in the previous chapter ... tension in the family, peer pressure, the lure of technology, building self-confidence, and working parents ... are equally relevant during the teenage years, with the suggestions regarding peer pressure and building self-confidence being especially important; the use of drugs as a result of peer pressure is obviously of great concern. The issue of being a working parent during these years, however, is not so much one of being there when your child comes home from school or during the summer ... as independence is a precious asset to a teenager ... but of being there for your child in the evenings and weekends. "Being there" means not being so tied up with or tired from ones work that one pays scant attention to the needs, often unspoken, of your children.

At the close of the teenage years, or shortly thereafter, there is a peer pressure issue that is so important, however, that it merits a few extra words ... the choice of career. When people sit down to think about what they want to do with their lives there are many factors that impact that decision. We live in a culture that bombards our senses constantly with messages about what is desirable, what is valued, which most of us have absorbed as if by osmosis.

In today's world, the most important factor that many people consider, albeit sometimes unconsciously, in choosing a career or livelihood is the amount of money they will make. It has become the number one cultural indicator of success and is of vital practical importance to those caught up in our consumer culture. While money is certainly indispensable for living, as discussed earlier, it is not the source of happiness that our culture leads us to believe it is. It should thus not be the driving force in your child's decision. The same holds true for the factor of status.

If your child is to be a happy adult, the task in approaching this decision is therefore to remove these cultural value judgments from the process to the extent possible so that your child can instead look solely at what is the right job/career for him or her. Each of us is different in terms of the things that interest us, the natural talents we have, the things that bring us satisfaction in their accomplishment. Since for most of us the time and effort we spend "working" exceeds anything else we do, it is important to our happiness that we choose an effort ... be it a career, or line of work, or unpaid effort ... that taps into our positive energy.

In our culture, so many people regardless of socio-economic status do not enjoy their work and see it as merely a means to an end ... making money, "putting food on the table." There is no joy in their work. This is a sad state of affairs because such people are being robbed of a source of happiness and self-worth.

Do not allow your child to fall into this trap. Help your child choose his or her effort, her career, carefully with their overall ... not just financial ... interests in mind.

For the remainder of this chapter I will deal solely with the one new factor that has thrust itself into the world of your teenage child ... sex. Not only is puberty arriving at an earlier age than decades ago, but sexual activity is common at an earlier age.

Parents need to be aware that it is the unusual teenager that has not had sexual intercourse during these years, and often with some frequency. And sex is no longer an expression of what one used to call "puppy love," but a detached exploration of the animal drive. The casual nature with which today's teenagers, male and female, often have sex with acquaintances as well as "friends with benefits" is a fact of life that a parent is at risk to ignore.

This is clearly an area where you as a parent need to decide where to draw the line. If you feel that teenagers should never have sex ... period ... then you have to find a way of communicating that to your child so that your position makes sense to him or her and evolves from your loving kindness and compassion. Laying down the law will not work.

But remember, the peer pressure to have sex will probably be great for both male and female teenagers today. It may be both wiser and more protective of your child's welfare to give your child the tools to both understand when it's ok or not to have sex and to make sure that when they do they do so safely. Regardless whether you choose to have this discussion with your child when it is younger or older, at some point you must accept your parental responsibility; you cannot allow your child's attitudes about sex to be formed by the prevailing culture and peer pressure if you care for your child's future well-being and happiness.

The Facts M'am, Just the Facts

It is the unusual situation where a teenager learns the facts of sex from his mother or father. There may be some minimal mention of the subject when parents feel their child is getting to that point in its life where something needs to be said, but often what is said is next to meaningless and makes parents look like fools in the eyes of their children. Instead, they learn from friends, books, magazines, movies … whatever.

It is very important for the future well-being of your children that they learn the facts of sex from you, their parent. There are several important reasons for this. You want to make sure that they have accurate information. You want to make sure that the information is presented within a healthy framework. And, most importantly perhaps, coming from you, the whole subject of sex will be taken out of the realm of exciting titillation and teenage rebellion.

If the school your children attend has sex education classes, that's great … if they're any good, that is. But even if they are, you cannot escape your responsibility as parent and you put your children in peril by leaving it to the school to educate your child on a subject so central to his or her future happiness.

If you are uncomfortable talking about this subject with your children, as many parents definitely are, get a book on the subject of sex education so that you can approach it in a professional manner. Remember, a little knowledge can be dangerous to your child. And although you may wish to leaven your discussion with examples from your own adolescence or young adulthood, do it in a way that does not make it seem to your children that this is a joking matter.

Beyond the Facts ... The Role of Sex

Before you can have a discussion with your child about not just the mechanics of sex but also how sex should be viewed, how it should be handled, what role it plays, you have to be clear in your own mind what you want to tell your child about sex. That statement may sound like a "no-brainer," but if your desire is to raise a happy child, then it requires some careful thought. So let me first explore the dynamics of healthy sex and its counterpart, unhealthy sex.

There's a reason why the expression is, "to lose oneself in the throes of passion," rather than, "to express love or affection through the throes of passion." It's not just that the former is more descriptive of how many people approach sex, it describes the basic problem in how we approach sex. While sex is a natural ingredient of a healthy life and relationship, it all too often is a key ingredient of an unhealthy life and relationship. What turns sex into one or the other?

The answer is, lust. Lust is a craving that has at its source a lack of equanimity, and certainly most of us, if we are honest, will admit that our sexual attractions and activities often derive from our insecurity, which is a lack of equanimity.

Many will counter that sex without lust is a boring, mechanical concept ... but that's not what I'm suggesting here. Remember, as discussed earlier, it's not about not having desire, it's about not having unskillful desires or cravings. Many will further defensively argue that sex is a biological necessity, a natural urge. While this is of course true, *when* one chooses to act on that urge is not a biological necessity, at least for humans. Instead, it is more often a psychological imperative.

For many people, sex is a form of validation to escape feelings of insecurity. For men, whether a teenager or adult, sex is often a way to project power ... indeed that is its evolutionary biological basis ... and yet the classic comic line, "How was it?" shows that for humans at least, behind the macho surface of the sex act is a deep sense of insecurity. For women, again for teenagers as well as adults, sex is often viewed as a tool to attract and keep a man. Although in today's world of casual sex or friends with benefits, it's not even about keeping a man; it's often just about peer pressure and being cool, desirable. Again, regardless of the role of sex in evolutionary biology, in humans it is typically evidence of a basic insecurity.

The result of this craving is that there is much sexual misconduct in the world, which leads to unhealthy lives and troubled relationships. But what exactly is sexual misconduct.

Some say it is defined by ones culture. While that may be true in a practical or legal sense, I would disagree with that from a spiritual perspective because there have been and are cultures, including ours, that condone or even encourage sexual activity which is harmful, at least psychologically, to the participants.

Since I am a Buddhist, if you ask how Buddhists define sexual misconduct that is not of much help either because the range of behaviors defined as sexual misconduct varies greatly. At one end of the spectrum, I once asked a monk what constitutes sexual misconduct and he said that as long as it was between consenting adults, sex was ok and there was no misconduct. At the other end of the spectrum is Thich Nhat Hanh, who has said that sex without love and a long-term commitment is sexual misconduct.[16]

In helping us navigate this question, I suggest that the primary moral principles of Buddhism, and most other religions, are very helpful ... treat others with respect and loving kindness and do others no harm, psychologically or physically. These will be our guiding principles.

In our culture, it is not unusual for teenage men, and increasingly women, to seek consensual sexual relationships that include:

- the very casual ... that is, one barely knows the other person;
- "friends with benefits"
- sex with various partners during the same period of time
- sex within a dating situation, and
- sex within a short-term committed relationship

If we look at these various situations from the perspective I propose, I would argue that casual sex, friends with benefits, and sex with various partners are all in this context, misconduct. While one can be kind in each of these situations, one cannot act with loving kindness or be truly thoughtful because typically one is acting from a lack of equanimity, one is focused on ones own needs and cravings. While the situations are indeed consensual, one or both partners are using the other to fill a craving and thus some

---

[16] Thich Nhat Hanh, *The Heart of the Buddha's Teaching,* Broadway Books, 1998, p.95

level of suffering is inevitable. Such free love is never really free.

As to sex in a dating situation or in a short-term committed relationship, the question is whether the sex is based on a craving, that is a lack of equanimity based on insecurity, or whether the sex flows from feelings of love or affection or fondness for the other person. If the latter, it is not misconduct; if the former, it is.[17]

To answer this question, people must look deep inside themselves and be very aware and honest, which for anyone let alone a teenager is difficult. If the answer is that the sex is based on a lack of equanimity, then not only should your child not have sex with this person, he or she needs to think carefully about the issue of sexual craving so that they are able to have healthy sexual relations in the future. They need to be adult about this; sex is not child's-play. Indeed, they need to be more adult and aware than most adults are.

If teenagers are able to be very mindful of the dynamics of the relationship and constantly remind themselves to think of their partner and not of themselves, they can approximate a caring relationship filled with loving kindness. But if they cannot do this, if they are acting out of insecurity and craving and only care for their partner because of what that person can do for them, then they cannot treat the person with loving kindness let alone really love someone. Until they master the art of loving/caring and approaching sex with equanimity they should thus not engage is sexual relations, since that would be sexual misconduct under the standards I have set.

If someone is not able to approach sex other than as a craving, they will only harm themselves and the other person. Explaining this to anyone, let alone a teenager, is not easy. It runs so counter to everything we learn in our

---

[17] You as parent may decide to place further restrictions on sex, but remember not to remove all freedom of action or display a lack of trust in your child.

culture and from out peers. But as a parent, you must find a way.

How you approach your child with this discussion will depend on the dynamics of your relationship. One suggestion ... if in the past you yourself have experienced pain as the result of sexual misconduct that you are able to share with your child, that would be a loving and effective way of communicating the importance of this subject and getting your child to stop and listen ... and think. But regardless whether you have a warm and loving, respectful relationship with your teenage child based on the lessons of this book or otherwise, or have a more typical love-frustration relationship with your teenage child, the importance of having this discussion cannot be overstated.

Chapter 8
Your Child, the Adult

If you've raised your children following the guidelines suggested in this book, you should have a wonderful relationship with them in their adulthood. Of course there will inevitably be occasional conflicts, but when they are always addressed within the context of unconditional love and compassion, they get voiced and resolved in a way that doesn't harm the relationship.

But what if you haven't raised your children in this way? What if you're reading this book when your children are already grown and the conflicts between you and your children are deeply rooted and there is either underlying tension or very visible tension between you whenever you get together? Or the conflicts are so bad that you don't even get together or possibly even speak?

It is almost never too late to address these conflicts and heal the relationship between you and your children. The reason is that all adults are still children who want to be loved unconditionally and respected by their parents.

The first step in the process is to look back over your relationship with your children, or it may just be one child with whom there is tension, with great clarity in light of what you have read in this book. This can be difficult, both in a practical sense and emotionally. But remember that the point is not to find fault with yourself but to understand that even a very well-meaning parent can do things which unintentionally harm their child. It is not your fault in a moral sense; it is a result of the way in which you were raised and the culture in which we live. But the parent is nevertheless almost always the immediate causal agent.

Once you have figured out what you did … it could be one thing, it could be many; it could have happened over a very short time frame or it could have been going on for years … the next step in the process is to make amends to your child or children.

Making amends … heartfully acknowledging that there are things you did which caused your child pain … will in most circumstances open the door to healthy communication and result in healing. There are three things that are critical when making amends: your acknowledgment must be unequivocal; state that however it may have appeared to your child you always loved your child and had his or her best interest at heart; and you must sincerely and abjectly apologize for the pain that you have cause your child over the years.

The best format to use when making amends is to start with a letter. By saying it in a letter rather than talking to your child, you will have the chance to review your words and make sure that you are communicating what you mean to communicate. It will also give your child a chance to digest what you have said.

Start the letter with something to the effect of, "I am writing to apologize for the pain I have caused you." Being upfront about the nature of the letter is critical to insuring that even if your relationship is very bad, possibly you are totally estranged, the letter will be read. Perhaps initially out of curiosity and disbelief. But if you have been very honest, open, and heartfelt in the letter, it will ultimately have the desired effect.

While it will be natural for you to want to explain why you did what you did … and this can greatly aid your child's healing … remember that it is critical that your acknowledgment must remain unequivocal. It cannot appear to your child that you are making excuses. Thus when you try to explain yourself it should be in the context of, "This does not excuse what I did, but it is important for you to know how this came to be." And then explain what ... whether it was something from your own upbringing or stress you were under at the time or whatever ... caused you to act as you did.

The reason why a carefully phrased explanation is important is that for your adult child to heal and forgive, your child needs to regain compassion for you. That compassion begins with remembering that parents are just human beings; we are a product of our upbringing and our culture. Often we do things with the best of intentions, but they turn out poorly and do harm. It is the rare parent that intentionally inflicts harm, psychological or otherwise, on his or her children. Also, being human, we often blurt out, especially in moments of anger or frustration, words that we really don't mean. But as the sign in my father's office used to say, "A word once spoken is like a stone thrown ... it cannot be recalled." The impact stays with us often for a lifetime.

Your letter should cause your child to think carefully about what really happened way back when that caused him or her to carry around so much pain. Chances are they will realize that their reaction to the events was caused by their inability as a child to correctly characterize the events and that when they now see them clearly for what they were, they will find it in their heart to forgive.

Let me briefly describe an example from my own life ... that is from my perspective as a child. For a variety of reasons that I briefly described in an earlier chapter, I came to feel unloved by my father as a child. The pain and insecurity that flowed from this feeling stayed with me for most of my adult life and caused me much suffering and a long-term history of serious social dysfunction. It was only much later in life that I came to understand that I, as a child, had misinterpreted these events as meaning that he didn't love me. But that was in fact not the case.

So strong was my emotional separation from my father that even when I received written evidence of his past love for me … this wasn't an amends letter, just regular correspondence, … it didn't even register. It was only after having come to understand the true facts that, after coming upon these letters by chance again while cleaning out my files one day, I realized the enormity of my error and the huge loss I had suffered as a result.

In addition to making amends, another way of helping your child heal these wounds is to practice *tonglen* on him or her. In an earlier chapter, I described how to practice *tonglen* on yourself to heal your relationship with yourself, to learn to love yourself unconditionally and have compassion for yourself. Here you would use the practice in the more common way, which is to receive another person's … in this instance your child's … pain and suffering, and send that person love, compassion, understanding, faith, and strength. I know it may well sound like new-age nonsense to you to apply this to someone else, rather than yourself, but I firmly believe that this can make a difference … for both you and your child.

Helping your child heal the rift between the two of you will be one of the most important things you have ever done for your child. Even if he or she has suffered much pain over the years, your child will finally come to know without any question that he was and is truly loved unconditionally. A more loving gift you could not give your child.

Epilogue

Life is a constant challenge because we, and the world we live in, are a function of two types of forces. One is evolutionary biology and the other is human psychology.

It is the rare individual ... whether religious or secular ... who has used the gift of the human mind to transcend our animal natures and has tried to build a world that is free of aggression and built instead on peaceful coexistence and love. Instead, man has used his powers of reason to make huge progress in the fields of science and other areas. Everything in our lives is new and modern and changing at an ever-increasing rate. But emotionally, we have not progressed much beyond our cave-dweller ancestors. If anything, in recent decades, we have become emotionally more conflicted as we have become more separated from the things that gave our forbears' lives meaning and stability.

Technology has not made our lives simpler, it has made them more complex. It has not lightened our workload, on balance, but created an environment where we have to be constantly "on." And our consumer-driven capitalist culture has created a mass of addicted people who are effectively controlled through ever-present marketing efforts.

This is the context that caused me to write this book. I do not pretend that anything I say or advocate will change the world we live in. That just isn't in the cards. But what I advocate can change the lives of your children and you, for I have attempted to provide you with a different perspective with which to view and interact with yourself, your children, and the world around you. Not one that separates you from the rest of society, but allows you to function mostly on

73

your terms true to your own self. If you build a world for yourself and your family filled with unconditional love and compassion, you and your family will experience peace and joy. You will be happy, even as the rest of the world continues on its unhappy, insecure way, consumed by neuroses that know no end.

I congratulate you on seeking to provide your children with a truly better life, not from a materialistic perspective but from a spiritual one ... happy and well adjusted. And in the process provide yourself with a better life as well.